READY, SET, CREATE!

WRITTEN BY
STEFFI CAVELL-CLARKE

Art Styles

KidHaven
PUBLISHING

Published in 2027 by
KidHaven Publishing, an Imprint of Greenhaven Publishing, LLC
2544 Clinton St., Buffalo, NY 14224

Written by: Steffi Cavell-Clarke
Edited by: Noah Leatherland
Designed by: Ker Ker Lee

Cataloging-in-Publication Data

Names: Cavell-Clarke, Steffi.
Title: Art styles / Steffi Cavell-Clarke.
Description: Buffalo, NY : KidHaven Publishing, 2027. | Series: Ready, set, create! | Includes glossary and index.
Identifiers: ISBN 9781534570139 (pbk.) | ISBN 9781534570146 (library bound) | ISBN 9781534570153 (ebook)
Subjects: LCSH: Art movements--Juvenile literature. | Art--History--Juvenile literature. | Art appreciation--Juvenile literature.
Classification: LCC N5308.C349 2027 | DDC 709--dc23

Printed in China

CPSIA compliance information: Batch #QS27KH: For further information contact Greenhaven Publishing LLC at 1-844-317-7404.

Please visit our website, www.greenhavenpublishing.com.
For a free color catalog of all our high-quality books, call toll free 1-844-317-7404 or fax 1-844-317-7405.

Find us on

Photo Credits – Images courtesy of Shutterstock.com, unless otherwise stated.

Cover & Recurring – Colorfuel Studio, DigitalShards, DenisProduction.com, OlScher. 2–3 – Nicky87. 4–5 – Sunny studio, T.Vyc. 6–7 – DC Studio, MaLija. 8–9 – Viacheslav Lopatin. 10–11 – Viacheslav Lopatin, Claude Monet, Public domain, via Wikimedia Commons. 12–13 – Rawpixel.com. 14–15 – Everett Collection, steve estvanik. 16–17 – Christian webster, Mark Green. 20–21 – Anton Vierietin, 365 Focus Photography spatuletail, Dominic Robinson from Bristol, UK, CC BY-SA 2.0, via Wikimedia Commons. 22–23 – Mayuberu, SeventyFour.

Contents

WORDS THAT LOOK LIKE THIS CAN BE FOUND IN THE GLOSSARY ON PAGE 24.

The Wonderful World of Art

Do you enjoy creating art? Making art is a great way to learn new skills, express your feelings, and use your amazing imagination. It can also make you think about the wonderful world around you.

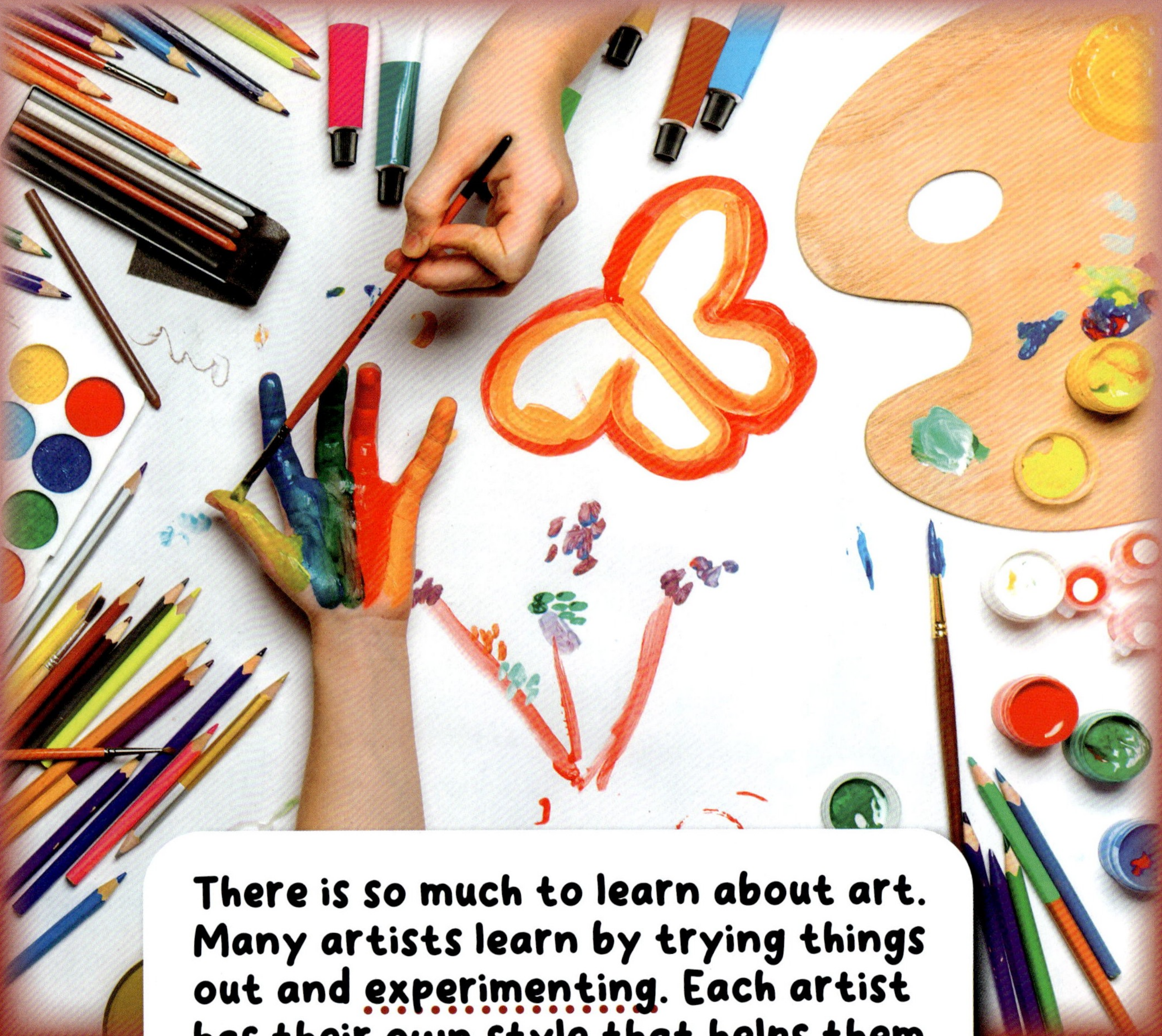

There is so much to learn about art. Many artists learn by trying things out and experimenting. Each artist has their own style that helps them create something special.

Art Styles

Art can look like lots of things, such as a painting, a sculpture, or a dance. Even paintings can look very different from one another. These different kinds of art are called styles.

Art styles change and evolve over time. Some use vibrant colors, and others use bold shapes. Let's take a look at some of the most popular art styles and see which ones you like best.

Renaissance Art

The Renaissance period lasted from around the 1300s to the 1600s CE. During this time, there were lots of new ideas and new art forms. Renaissance artists often focused on making their art look as real as possible.

The School of Athens
by Raphael

Leonardo da Vinci was an artist, inventor, and scientist from the Renaissance period. He painted one of the world's most famous paintings. It is called the *Mona Lisa*.

Impressionism

An "impression" is an idea of what something or someone is like. Impressionism is an art style that tries to capture a single moment, as if it is happening right in front of you.

Springtime
by Claude Monet

Claude Monet was a famous Impressionist artist. He used dots and dabs of paint to create a sense of movement in his paintings. This painting is called *Woman with a Parasol.*

CAN YOU SEE HOW THE DRESS SEEMS TO BE MOVING IN THE WIND?

Cubism

Cubism is an art style that uses shapes such as squares, triangles, and rectangles. Cubist art shows objects or people from many different positions at the same time.

Still Life with a Guitar
by Juan Gris

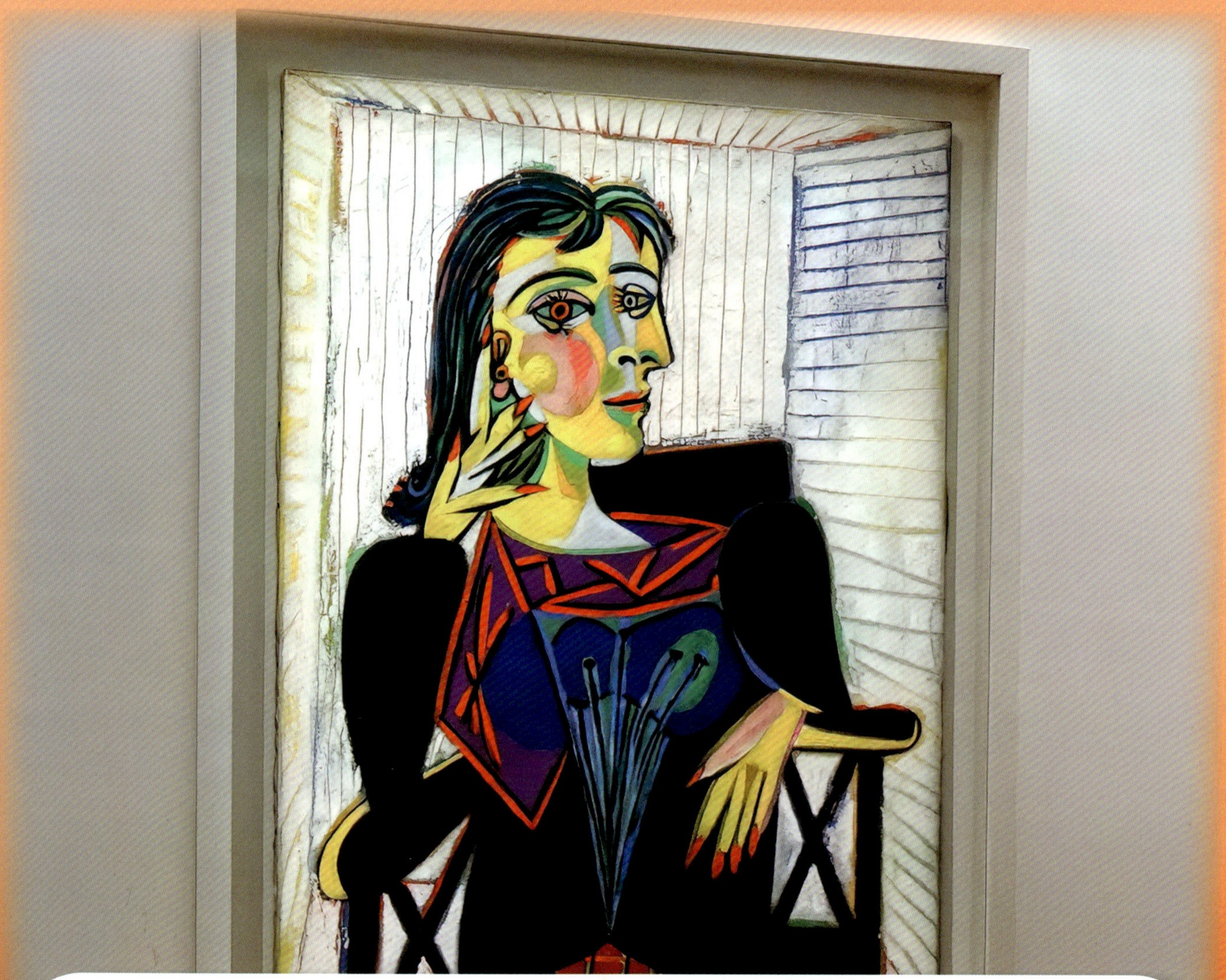

Pablo Picasso was one of the artists who started Cubism. He experimented with colors, shapes, and lines. He painted faces as if you could see all their different sides at once.

Surrealism

Surrealism is an art style that creates images that you would not see in real life. They are often inspired by dreams. They might not look like anything you have seen before.

Salvador Dalí was famous for making dreamlike pieces. He created surreal scenes and combined things that you would not expect to see together. This is one of his works, called *Lobster Telephone*.

Abstract Art

Abstract art uses colors, lines, and shapes without showing real people or objects. Instead, it creates feelings, energy, and movement in a fun and creative way.

Composition VII
by Wassily Kandinsky

Wassily Kandinsky was a famous abstract artist. Many of his paintings were inspired by music. He thought about how the music made him feel. He used those thoughts and feelings to paint colorful shapes.

Yellow-Red-Blue
by Wassily Kandinsky

Pop Art

Pop Art is a colorful and modern style of art. It uses bright colors and pictures from everyday life. The "pop" in Pop Art comes from the artists taking things from pop culture.

Andy Warhol was one of the most famous Pop Art artists. In his art, he made many versions of the same image. He turned everyday objects into bold works of art.

Campbell's Soup Cans
by Andy Warhol

Unique Art Styles

Many artists explore different styles to find the one that feels right for them. Some artists develop a unique style that shows off their personality and creativity.

BANKSY BECAME FAMOUS THROUGH THEIR STREET ART.

Frida Kahlo was famous for painting women to show how strong and powerful they are. She painted many colorful self-portraits that expressed her feelings, culture, and love for nature.

Me and My Parrots
by Frida Kahlo

Ready, Set, Create!

The world of art is full of color, fun, and surprise. Every time you create, you are telling a story only you can tell.

A great way to practice different art styles is to simply try them. It can be a painting, drawing, or any kind of art that you like. So, gather your art materials, and start exploring!

Glossary

evolve to change and develop over time

experimenting exploring and trying new things

inventor someone who makes new things

modern to do with recent or present times

pop culture popular things that are enjoyed by lots of people, such as books, movies, TV shows, and music

positions places where things are

self-portraits pictures someone creates of themselves

vibrant bright and bold

Index